VIPER
PURE PERFORMANCE BY DODGE

BY THE AUTO EDITORS OF CONSUMER GUIDE®

Publications
International, Ltd.

ACKNOWLEDGEMENTS
The editors gratefully acknowledge the Viper's four executive "fathers" for their time, recollections and
insights: Robert A. Lutz, President, Chrysler Corporation; Francois J. Castaing, Vice-President, Vehicle
Engineering; Thomas C. Gale, Vice-President, Product Design; and Carroll Shelby, Performance
Consultant. Special appreciation to Viper Project Manager Roy H. Sjoberg, Viper Project Synthesis
Herb Helbig, Viper Engine Manager James A. Royer, and other members of Team Viper for sharing their
experiences. Special thanks to Barbara Fronczak and Brandt Rosenbush, Chrysler Historical Collection.
Also thanks to Debbie Anderson, Thomas J. Kowaleski, Erika Huyck, Christine Pikulas and the entire
Chrysler Public Relations Staff for their invaluable assistance in preparing this volume. And to Alex
Gabbard for technical assistance regarding the AC Shelby Cobra 427.

PHOTO CREDITS
Many thanks to our exceptionally fine photographers, without whose assistance this book would
not be possible: **Roland Flessner**—78, 79; **Alex Gabbard**—64, 66 (AC Shelby Cobra 427); **Sam
Griffith**—19, 64, 66 (Corvette); **Jerry Heasley**—46, 47, 48, 49, 51, 52, 53; **Hidden Image**—45;
Joe Joliet—25, 36, 40, 41, 44, 45, 54; **Vince Manocchi**—18, 19, 24, 25, 26, 27, 58, 59, 61, 64,
68, 70, 71, 73, 76, 77.

OWNER CREDITS
Special thanks to the owners of the cars featured in this book for their enthusiastic cooperation. They are
listed below along with the page number on which their cars appear: **William E. True**—18; **Paul
Bastista**—18; **Peter Bogard**—19; **Allen Cummins**—19; **Charles A. Vance**—19; **Carroll Shelby**—19.

CONTENTS

It's one of the most talked-about cars of the last quarter-century—and one of the most exciting, too. Consider what it's been called: a "Cobra for the '90s," the "process blueprint" for every Chrysler Corporation car that follows it, a beast, "retro," a stunning achievement, the kind of car you weren't supposed to be able to build anymore, a symbol of Detroit's resurgence against the Japanese onslaught—and a sure-fire future collector's item. It's the Dodge Viper RT/10, and this is its story.

Or rather, stories. For Viper is more than just a burly, limited-production, "back-to-basics" high-performance sports car. It is unquestionably one of those memorable machines that comes along but once in a generation. And it's just as much a bold experiment, pioneering not only several new technologies but a new approach for Chrysler in bringing cars to market, one that bodes well for the company's future.

That approach, which Chrysler calls a "platform team," isn't a new idea, just a very logical one. And it works splendidly. As you'll read in these pages, the Viper sped from auto-show concept to showroom reality at the hyperlight velocity

usually associated with Japanese products: a mere three years. And that's significant. If anyone continues to doubt that American automakers can still react to market demands as swiftly and correctly as foreign competitors, the Viper erases those thoughts conclusively.

Not that the car itself is all that commercially vital to Chrysler. High-buck sports machines built in annual lots of but a few thousand have never made up the bottom-line difference for an automaker's survival. The Avanti, for instance, couldn't prevent Studebaker from going under in the '60s, and today's ZR-1 has done nothing to revitalize Corvette sales at Chevrolet. But as both symbol and prototype for Chrysler's new way of doing business, the Viper is well-nigh perfect. And happily, its lessons have been applied to cars that *do* make a difference to Chrysler today and tomorrow, such as in the well-received 1993 "LH" sedan trio of Chrysler Concorde, Dodge Intrepid, and Eagle Vision.

So the Viper is nothing if not historic. Of course, it is not Chrysler's first production two-seater. That distinction is reserved for the dubious Chrysler's TC by Maserati of 1989-90, which owes more to the several famous Ghia-

built show cars designed by Virgil Exner in the 1950s (detailed in Chapter 1). But Viper is definitely the first true sports car from America's number-three automaker. It's also Detroit's most potent production car since the last Hemi-engine MoPars and big-block Corvettes of the early '70s, and arguably the most elemental sports car since the great Shelby-Cobras.

Which brings up another point. In today's restrictive, highly regulated automotive world, it's more than faintly amazing that Chrysler would dare a Cobra-type machine. The odds against it were simply too great, or so said the pundits. Imagine: a 400-horsepower V-10 car that seats only two, rates as a "gas guzzler" under federal fuel-economy rules, lacks the almost mandatory modern safety features of airbag and antilock brakes, and makes do with side curtains, a skimpy top, and no outside door handles. Just getting it past the Washington czars for safety, emissions, noise, and mileage would be difficult, if not impossible, right? And who out there in buyerland would actually lay out good money for such an impractical thing, especially at a hefty $50,000?

Ah, but the pundits didn't count

on the skill and tenacity of Chrysler executives, designers, and engineers, nor on the lust for speed and style that still beats in so many enthusiast hearts. Viper stands as eloquent testimony to both: a car whose reason for being is simply that some people knew it *should* be, and practicality be damned.

The following chapters detail not only how Viper was created but why, and in the best possible way: via the words of its "four fathers." These are Robert A. Lutz, President of Chrysler Corporation; Francois J. Castaing, Vice-President, Vehicle Engineering; Thomas C. Gale, Vice-President, Product Design; and Carroll Shelby, Performance Consultant. That Shelby was involved is no coincidence. Viper is the car he'd been wanting to build since his final Cobras. An old friend from Shelby's association with Ford, Lee Iacocca, helped make sure it came out right before retiring as Chrysler chairman at the end of 1992.

But many others also had a hand in making Viper the modern thriller it is. Lutz, for example, is not only an avid enthusiast but a Cobra owner, an expert high-performance driver, and one of the most worldly wise auto executives around, having worked at both

BMW and Ford Europe. Castaing, with his considerable Formula 1 experience at Renault, was an ideal choice to direct Viper's overall engineering. And he picked an equally able team leader in ex-GM engineer Roy H. Sjoberg, who had worked on mid-engine Corvette experiments and thus knew more than a few things about high-performance sports cars. Gale is not only one of the most talented designers in the business but one of the few with a business background.

Then there are all the members of Team Viper: the experts in manufacturing, materials, plant management, and other disciplines who not only had to make a dream come true but do so with a speed and economy unheard-of at Chrysler or anywhere else in Detroit. That they succeeded so brilliantly testifies as much to their enthusiasm and dedication as to their considerable talents.

There's a lot more to say about the Viper—and you'll read it in these pages: all the colorful stories from the casual beginnings of this car through its stunning premiere and on to rip-roaring real-world road-burner. And we're glad to report that there are more stories to come. As you'll read, Chrysler

foresees a long life for Viper—perhaps as much as 10 years—and is planning some tantalizing "enhancements" for the near future.

For now, settle back and enjoy the high-powered excitement and drama that have already made this automobile the stuff of legends. They said it couldn't be done, but Viper is here, and it's more than ample reason for we who love cars to rejoice—not just about what Chrysler has wrought but the future of that company and, we hope, all of Detroit.

The editors gratefully acknowledge the Viper's four executive "fathers" for giving so generously of their time, recollections, and insights: Robert A. Lutz, President; Francois J. Castaing, Vice-President, Vehicle Engineering; Thomas C. Gale, Vice-President, Product Design; and Carroll Shelby, Performance Consultant. Special appreciation to Viper Project Manager Roy H. Sjoberg and other members of Team Viper for sharing their experiences. Finally, thanks to Thomas J. Kowaleski, Erika Huyck, Christine Pikulas, and the entire Chrysler Public Relations Staff for their invaluable assistance in preparing this book.

Viper was born as a "concept car," a one-of-a-kind "what if?" machine. It was designed to draw crowds at auto shows while gauging public response to new styling and engineering ideas, some of which might be edging toward production. Show cars have long been an auto industry staple, and Chrysler has shown its fair share of what it once termed "idea cars." Many of these were open two-seaters that looked sporty but were far more lush and complex than "pure" sports cars like MG.

Chrysler's first such experiment appeared back in 1940, when the creators of the far-distant future Viper were hardly out of short pants. This was the Thunderbolt, a long, low, two/three-seat convertible styled by Alex Tremulis of Briggs Manufacturing Company, which then supplied most of Chrysler's production bodies. It was nicknamed the "push-button car" for its several electrically operated features, including door and trunklid releases (via solenoids), window lifts (electro-hydraulic), and a novel metal top that stowed out of sight behind the cockpit. Styling was of the "bathtub school" favored in the final years before World War II, with rounded contours, skirted wheels, and (another novelty) hidden headlamps. A wide bright molding along the rocker panels suggested a "bumper."

Thunderbolt was conceived mainly as a showroom traffic-builder, and the LeBaron custom bodyworks, another longtime Chrysler supplier, built six for coast-to-coast display at selected dealers during 1941. Though trimmed and painted somewhat differently, all

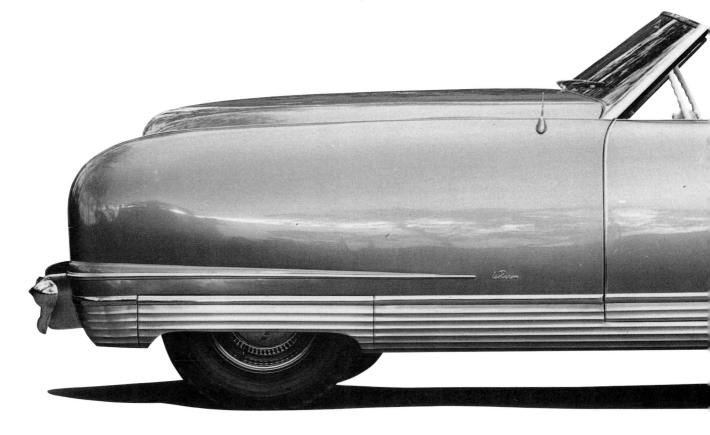

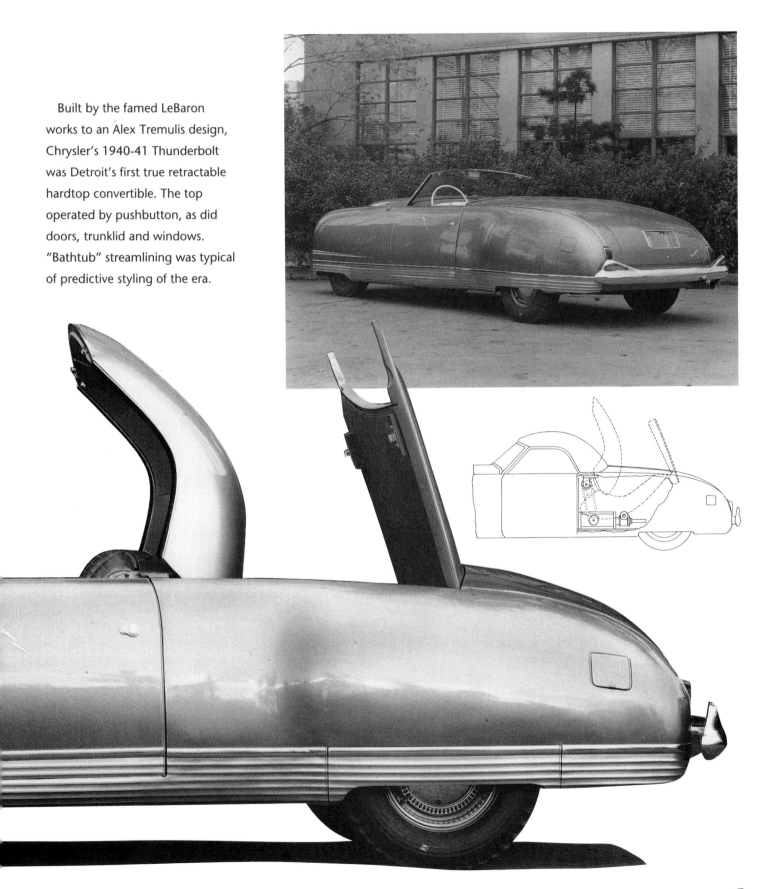

Built by the famed LeBaron works to an Alex Tremulis design, Chrysler's 1940-41 Thunderbolt was Detroit's first true retractable hardtop convertible. The top operated by pushbutton, as did doors, trunklid and windows. "Bathtub" streamlining was typical of predictive styling of the era.

featured leather cockpits, edge-lighted Lucite gauges, and 127.5-inch-wheelbase chassis from Chrysler's contemporary Saratoga/New Yorker. Powerplant was a 140-horsepower 323.5-cubic-inch straight eight mated to Fluid Drive semi-automatic transmission. Four Thunderbolts survive today.

Chrysler didn't again toy with two-seaters until the mid-Fifties. By that time, its milestone Hemi V-8, introduced in the 1951 Chryslers, had attracted wealthy sportsman Briggs Cunningham, whose two

Cadillac-powered entries had run 10th and 11th in the 1950 edition of the punishing 24 Hours of Le Mans in France. Knowing the potent, compact Hemi was perfect for a sports car, Cunningham set up shop in Palm Beach, Florida, and turned out a handful of fast, fleet-looking, fastidiously crafted Hemi-powered sports cars.

The most numerous were tagged C-3: a 2+2 cabriolet and Continental coupe derived from Briggs' 1951-52 C-1 and C-2 open sports-racers. Bearing smooth, shapely bodies designed and built

by Italy's house of Vignale, C-3s rode wheelbases of 105 or 107 inches and used strong ladder-type steel-tube chassis with all-coil suspension (via Ford twin A-arms fore and Chrysler live axle aft), big drum brakes and, of course, the brilliant 331-cid hemispherical-head V-8.

Packing bhp that ranged from 220 to 235, the C-3 could see a genuine 120 mph and do 0-60 in 8 seconds or less. But its real purpose was to qualify Cunningham for production-class racing, which Briggs pursued with his open C-4R, C-4RK, C-5R, and C-6R. At well over $10,000, the C-3 was far too costly for anything but very limited sale, and only 18 coupes and nine cabrios were built, all between 1952 and '55. A pity there weren't more. They were glorious.

Looking like a cross between an early-Fifties Ferrari Barchetta and some later Chrysler show cars, the Hemi-powered Cunningham C-2R sports-racer can be considered a "grandfather" of the modern Dodge Viper. Only three were built, all in 1952-53.

Back at Chrysler, the Hemi, despite its undoubted performance, did nothing to stem the sharp sales slide that began with the end of the postwar boom market in 1950. Dull styling and dowdy image were the main problems. But help was at hand in the form of aggressive new managers led by president L.L. "Tex" Colbert, who enticed the talented Virgil Exner from Studebaker to head Highland Park design.

While doing what he could to spruce up 1952-54 styling, Ex conjured a series of "idea cars" to perk public interest in Chrysler design pending the flashy all-new showroom models being readied for 1955. Most of these exercises were built by Ghia of Italy, and were large, luxurious four-seaters and 2+2s. But European sports cars had come to fascinate Americans,

and though their sales were always low, their interest value was high. As a result, Detroit rushed out a slew of sporty two-seaters in the early and mid-Fifties—mostly show cars, but also a few you could buy, like the 1951-54 Nash-Healey and 1954 Kaiser-Darrin. One 1953 showmobile ended up spawning the most enduring American sports car of all: the Chevrolet Corvette.

Not unexpectedly, Chrysler stoked the public's "sports car fever" with its own two-seat dreams, but these were more

Despite its badge, the 1954 Plymouth Belmont rode a Dodge Royal V-8 chassis. Briggs Manufacturing Company designed and built this open two-seater, partly to interest Chrysler in using fiberglass bodywork for production cars. A showroom version was never seriously contemplated.

"personal" concepts like Ford's first Thunderbird of 1955. An example is the Belmont, designed and built in 1954 by Briggs Manufacturing on a 114-inch Dodge chassis, even though this was a publicity exercise for Plymouth. Clean, if slightly lumpy, the Belmont was not particularly radical except for its fiberglass body, then still a novelty. It thus departed from Exner's Ghia-built exercises rendered in steel, though it followed most of them in being fully driveable.

Originally painted metallic blue, the Belmont had a fabric top, high door sills, and white-leather bucket seats with a dividing armrest concealing radio and power antenna controls. A very wide dummy hood scoop sat above a Nash-like grille flanked by headlights nestled in jumbo

chromed bezels. Beneath the hood lurked Dodge's lively new 241-cid "Red Ram" hemi V-8 with 150 bhp, linked to Hy-Drive semi-automatic. But though the Belmont looked ready to go after the Corvette/Kaiser-Darrin market, that market was too tiny to bother with, and the car itself was a technical and stylistic dead end.

An ultimately more significant effort was the Exner-designed Dodge Firearrow series. There were four in all. The first was a sleek, two-place metallic-red roadster mockup built in 1953 with 115-inch wheelbase, unframed windshield, and a big square grille bisected by a blade-type bumper that fully encircled the body. Quad headlamps, destined to be featured on most every U.S. production car by 1958, rode very low beneath the bumper.

The following year, Ghia built a running version of this design. Painted yellow and sometimes called "Firearrow II," it mounted a 119-inch '54 Dodge Royal V-8 chassis and bore a few appearance changes evidently aimed at greater on-road practicality. The main alteration was single headlamps moved up to faired-in fender pods, plus functional quad exhaust pipes exiting the body in stacked pairs behind the rear wheels. There were now no bumpers as such, but vestiges of the previous perimeter theme remained in a large black-finished horizontal grille bar and single wide chrome/black side moldings. There was still no top, but the interior was fully trimmed in saddle-grain black leather. Luggage stowed behind the

cockpit, the spare in a separate compartment further aft. As on all running Firearrows, this roadster carried a production 241 Dodge Red Ram V-8, as well as Chrysler's then-new fully automatic two-speed PowerFlite transmission.

Two additional Firearrows were shown later in 1954: a metallic-blue 2+2 sport coupe ("III") and a bright-red four-place convertible ("IV"), also on 119-inch '54 Dodge chassis. Both wore evolutionary styling marked by wrapped windshields (fully framed on the ragtop), inboard quad headlamps astride fully open grilles, and short, vertical bumperettes front and rear. Betty Skelton drove the coupe to a new closed-course world speed record for women of 143.44 mph. The convertible, meantime, went

Built by Ghia to Virgil Exner's designs, the 1953-54 Dodge Firearrow foursome included two roadsters with unique frameless windshields, plus 2+2 coupe and four-seat convertible. The second roadster (*below left*) was fully operational. So was the convertible (*below*) that led to the later Dual-Ghia.

on to inspire the limited-production 1956-58 Dual-Ghia, spearheaded by Detroit trucking magnate Eugene Casaroll. Happily, all the running Firearrows survive today, fully restored after rescue from one-time oblivion by the Bortz Auto Collection in Highland Park, Illinois, near Chicago.

Chrysler showed two more sporting ideas in 1954, and although they led to nothing, they deserve mention. The prettier one was the Plymouth Explorer, a metallic-green coupe *a la* closed Firearrow on a 114-inch '54 Plymouth chassis (complete with plodding 110-bhp 230-cid L-head six). It was easily spotted by a huge mushroom-shaped vertical-bar grille, large single headlamps set inboard of more fulsome front fenders, and elevated rear flanks suggesting fins.

The Dodge Granada was something else. Suggested by division chief Bill Newberg, this was another sporty four-seat ragtop on a '54 Dodge Royal V-8 chassis, but the styling of its fiberglass body was dubious at best. Nobody except Newberg really liked it, least of all Virgil

Exner, who had almost nothing to do with the ungainly design. The front was especially contrived. The Bortz Collection has also rescued this experimental—mainly, one thinks, for history's sake.

More pleasing by far was Exner's 1955 Falcon, an open "personal" two-seater on a trim 105-inch wheelbase. Its large, square

The Ghia-built '54 Plymouth Explorer (*center and opposite*) echoed the svelte Firearrow coupe, but had a pedestrian six-cylinder Plymouth chassis. Ragtop '54 Dodge Granada (*above and top*) boasted a lively Red Ram V-8, but also a contrived fiberglass body.

eggcrate grille, blade bumpers, side exhaust pipes, and relatively large wheels reflected Ex's fondness for "classic" design themes, as did the rakish long-hood/short-deck proportions. Construction was unitized steel, with what Chrysler called a "cellular platform frame structure." Power came from a 331 Hemi tuned for some 225 bhp and again linked to PowerFlite. A manual soft top stowed beneath a Corvette-type hard cover. The Falcon would have been a perfect reply to Ford's T-Bird, but again, Chrysler just couldn't see it.

Nor was Chrysler sold on the two-place Plymouth XNR roadster of 1960, one of Ex's last major Chrysler dreams. Utilizing the six-cylinder chassis of the firm's then-new Valiant compact, the XNR (for "Exner") explored competition-inspired asymmetric design with its prominent hood scoop, tailfin, and bubble windscreen— all set firmly left. A hard tonneau clipped in to cover the passenger's seat. With all this, the XNR was as close as Chrysler ever came to a pure sports car—until Viper.

Opposite page: Exner's '55 Falcon would have made a great Thunderbird-fighter, but was strictly for show. Exposed side exhausts prefigure those on today's Viper. *This page:* 1960 Plymouth XNR bore "asymmetric" design. Big tailfin formed a headrest for the driver. Hard tonneau clipped in over the passenger's seat.

PRODUCTION
TWO-SEATERS

This page: Sports cars were great crowd-pullers in the Fifties, but only giant General Motors was able to make real money with one. Even then, the original Chevrolet Corvette of 1953 almost expired two years later for lack of sales. At the other extreme, faltering Kaiser tried a fiberglass sports car in 1954, but the unique sliding-door Kaiser-Darrin (based on the compact Henry J chassis) did nothing to keep its maker alive, and only 435 were built. Ford fared far better with its 1955 Thunderbird, a "personal car" that outsold the Vette 16 to 1. Yet even that didn't satisfy Dearborn bean-counters, so the Bird ballooned into a four-seater after 1957 and sold better still. *Opposite page:* Corvette became a genuine world-class high-performance sports car after '55. The fuel-injected '57s and the 1963-67 Sting Rays have long been among the most coveted models, but the subsequent 1968-82 "Shark" series and the current 1984 generation, exemplified by the high-tech ZR-1, have their share of fans. Even more revered—and precious—are Carroll Shelby's great Sixties Cobras, stark British-built AC roadsters stuffed with Ford 289 and 427 V-8s. Incredibly fast and hairy to handle, the uncompromising Cobra directly inspired the Dodge Viper, with Shelby himself acting as its "spiritual conscience."

CHAPTER TWO

Straight from the Heart

The Viper is a parade all by itself.

It rolls by like a break in the routine, a celebrity glimpsed in the flesh, a brassy "Stars and Stripes Forever." Folks nudge and point. Whooping kids pedal their bikes like mad, trying to keep up.

Heads turn and trace the car's passage into the distance. In its wake a void is created, the street no longer a stage.

The spectacle lasts longer from behind the wheel.

A turn of the key ignites eight liters of aluminum V-10. Exhaust

pipes bark just below your elbow. Engage the clutch. Prod the accelerator. At just 1200 rpm there are 400 pounds/feet of torque at your command. It pours forth like water over Niagara Falls.

Hit it!

Reverberations from the side pipes send roosting birds heavenward. The massive hood quivers, the steering wheel comes to life. Wind tattoos your scalp. Dig deeper into the throttle. Aim down the straight. Get on the brakes. Bend the Viper into a turn.

Feel the tires bite. Accelerate out of the corner. Your eyes are barely three feet above the pavement rushing by. A vortex of dust and leaves swirls from the tail. Shift! Accelerate! Do it again.

Inside or out, few cars are so provocative. The Viper RT/10 has all-independent suspension, but no anti-lock brakes or driver-side air bag. Its 400-bhp 488-cid V-10 and 6-speed manual gearbox net 0-60 mph in 4.4 seconds and a 163 mph top speed.

Cars like this are rare. And cars like this from an American automaker are almost unheard of. But Chrysler has one in the Viper. And it's no accident.

From its inception, Viper's mission was to resurrect the excitement of the very boldest of sports cars, the fabled AC Shelby Cobra 427. It is, in fact, Cobra–like in conception—a pure two seater with rear-wheel drive and big-cube power—and in detail—side curtains instead of roll-up windows, and no exterior door handles.

At the same time it is amassing the lore that is essential to making cars like the Cobra larger than life.

The Viper saga began in early 1988, as some of Chrysler Corporation's top decision makers, who also happen to be car guys, turned to the notion of building a new car with the spirit of the original 1965-1967 Cobra.

Chrysler's design staff jumped at the assignment. Their sketches became a concept car—one that dazzled auto show audiences. People wrote letters asking Chrysler, "Build it, please!" Some actually sent deposit checks. Suddenly, a car company barely registering a heartbeat had a

"A Cobra for the '90s"

ROBERT A. LUTZ
President, Chrysler Corporation

Conventional Detroit wisdom holds that "car guys" with solid business experience make the best corporate leaders. Chrysler President Bob Lutz is a "car guy" of international experience and renown.

Born in Switzerland to American parents, Lutz was a U.S. Marine Corps pilot in the late '50s, attaining the rank of captain. He then earned an MBA from the University of California-Berkeley in 1962 before starting his automotive career at General Motors, which he served most notably as head of its German Opel subsidiary. Next came three years at BMW as Executive Vice-President for Sales and member of the Munich automaker's Board of Directors.

In 1974, Lutz was named president of Ford Europe. In addition to holding a seat on the board, he served executive vice-presidencies at Ford's International and Truck Operations. He joined Chrysler Motors as Executive Vice-President in mid-1986, and become President-Operations two years later. He subsequently become Chrysler Motors president and, in January 1991, president of Chrysler Corporation.

An expert driver, Lutz loves fast cars. He owns a Cobra, so it's no surprise that he not only suggested the Viper as a "Cobra for the '90s," but backed it all the way. The result? "The U.S. car industry had this deplorable reputation of being out-maneuvered by the Japanese at every turn," he said. "We couldn't do anything fast or new or exciting. The Viper, with one blow, has made all that go away . . . . This is a car only Americans could do. We had the history that was able to generate the nostalgia, which was part of the creative force behind the car."

Preserved Viper's Looks

THOMAS C. GALE
Vice-President, Product Design

You've seen the design talents of Tom Gale reflected in Chrysler cars ranging from the 1987-generation LeBaron coupe and convertible to the fabulous new Dodge Viper RT/10. But Gale is unique among automotive design directors in playing a dual role within his organization. He's not only Vice-President for Product Design, but General Operations Manager for Chrysler's trend-setting, hot-selling minivans.

It was the minivan's high commercial acceptance and corporate importance that prompted Chrysler's first thoughts of reorganizing its various vehicle programs around multi-discipline "platform teams." As a small-scale project, Viper was an ideal testbed for the concept, and quickly proved its value—so much so that all Chrysler programs are now organized along essentially the same lines.

Gale was an ideal choice to wear both design and managerial hats,

earning Master's degrees from Michigan State University in Arts (1967) and Business Administration (1978). Joining Chrysler in 1967, he held a variety of posts in Advance Body Engineering and car/truck design through 1981. He also served as a product planning analyst in 1976-77. Gale was named Director of Interior Design in 1981 and Director of Exterior Design the following year. He became Vice-President of Design in April 1985, adding General Manager-Minivan responsibilities in January 1991.

Like most everyone connected with the Viper, Gale is passionate about automobiles. And his tastes are eclectic, running from hot pickups (he drives a custom Dodge Dakota) to street rods.

He's also an accomplished test driver, and one of his "kicks" about Project Viper was being able to participate as such. "It was fun, especially because of the enthusiasm we all felt for it," he said. "When people know the bosses are behind something—that we're going to work late nights and on weekends, or go to the proving grounds to thrash something to make it right—they come to it with a whole new perspective. I mean, when the design guy—me—gets invited out to the proving grounds to do the handling course, that's total involvement. And that's what it takes."

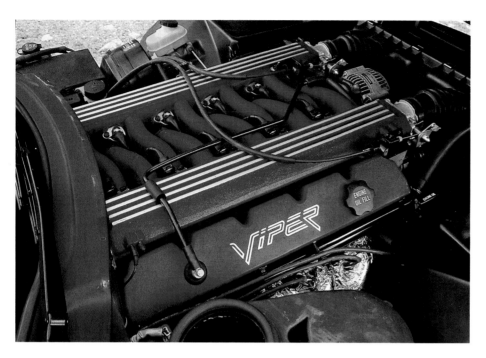

by announcing that the Japanese-built Dodge Stealth would pace the 1991 Indianapolis 500, it was Viper that raced to the rescue. Another prototype was hurriedly produced and pressed into pace-car service. At the wheel was the man behind the legend, Carroll Shelby, who just months before had undergone a heart transplant. Shelby was the father of the Cobra, and a driving force in the development of the Viper.

When the first half-dozen of the 200 1992 production models rolled into Southern California showrooms in May, they caused a sensation. Ecstatic Dodge dealers accepted orders at triple the $50,000 list price. Others said their Viper was not for sale at any price—it was too valuable a drawing card.

high-profile hit on its hands.

Within Chrysler's ranks an elite commando unit of car engineers and designers was formed. Equipment was "borrowed," space "procured." This group produced a running prototype in just 11 months.

Lee Iacocca himself is said to have authorized production of the Viper after an awesome test blast down a suburban Detroit street.

And when Chrysler stumbled into a public-relations briar patch

Viper's Technical Overseer

FRANCOIS J. CASTAING
Vice-President, Vehicle Engineering

When Chrysler Corporation bought American Motors in 1987, it "inherited" engineer Francois Castaing, one of AMC's most valuable assets and a man who would play a pivotal role in Project Viper. He joined Chrysler as Vice-President of Jeep and Truck Engineering, then in late 1989 was named to head all vehicle engineering activities.

A 1968 graduate of the *Ecole Nationale Supérieure d'Arts et Metiers* in his native France, Castaing came to AMC in 1980 from its then-new partner Renault. He had spent 10 years at that state-owned giant,

heading development and engine design for Renault's Gordini specialty-car subsidiary. In 1975, he advanced to chief engineer for its Formula 1 racing program. His first task at AMC was supervising the launch of the Franco-American Alliance subcompact, a literal transatlantic career bridge. He subsequently held a variety of top-echelon AMC development and engineering positions.

Castaing says of Project Viper: "It's been an experiment in many ways. If you think about it, it's unique for a major manufacturer to build a one-of-a-kind car, show it to the public and then say, 'If you like it, we'll make it for you.' The idea of doing it with a small 'skunkworks' type team was another experiment, with everyone in the same room working together. It was an experiment in that we took volunteers; we selected people for their enthusiasm. And it was an experiment in some new technologies . . . . But I believe we kept to the spirit of the car all the way."

Eager enthusiasts bid triple the Viper's $50,000 list price to be among the first in line for the ride of a lifetime.

Still, the Viper has critics. It's been labeled irresponsible—a poor use of both natural resources *and* Chrysler's resources. Some say a company in Chrysler's financial condition ought to have introduced a mass-market subcompact. It's been branded an extravagance born of outsized egos—a low-volume mega-buck plaything.

For its part, Chrysler says Viper helped them fine tune the "team" concept used to develop the new LH family of sedans, cars widely regarded as vital to the company's very survival as an automaker. In addition, project Viper pioneered fresh ways of dealing with suppliers—techniques that will help lower costs on the line of Chrysler subcompacts due in the mid-1990s.

As well, Chrysler points out that the Viper itself is a testbed for new body-panel modeling processes, a new fuel-injection system, and a new transmission. The car also introduces a Chrysler-patented single-piece windshield frame and is the first U.S.-built car to employ urethane foam interior trim that's actually a structural component.

Still, Viper's essence isn't to be found in a board room, or technical specification, or even 0-60 mph times. Much about this car has to do with desire and sheer sensation.

Indeed, it has otherwise straight-laced Chrysler officials making dreamy analogies; one said it recaptures the perfection of young love.

A more down-to-earth view of Viper might be that it marks the return of automotive enthusiasts to Chrysler's helm—men and women with an appreciation of engineering and performance. Moreover, it shows that an American automaker can respond quickly to market desires with a car that invigorates the soul and obliterates the routine.

The Conscience of Viper

**CARROLL SHELBY
Performance Consultant**

Car lovers everywhere revere Carroll Shelby for giving us some of history's greatest high-performance cars. A flight instructor in World War II, then oil-field roustabout and, he admits, "rotten chicken rancher," Shelby began racing cars in 1952 (at a relatively late age 29). Turning professional two years later, he ultimately drove for Ferrari and Aston-Martin, scored numerous wins in Europe, and copped three U.S. driving titles before heart trouble forced a premature end to his driving career in 1960.

But new and even greater triumphs lay ahead. In 1961, Shelby put Ford's then-new small-block V-8 into the lithe British AC roadster to create the legendary Shelby Cobra 260/289, followed by the almighty big-block Shelby Cobra 427 in 1965. He also spearheaded Ford's mid-decade assault on Le-Mans, managing a team of GT40s to twin victories in 1966-67. And somehow, he found time to turn Ford's Mustang ponycar into the exciting semi-competition GT-350/GT-500 of 1965-70.

Shelby then left the car manufacturing business to market his own custom wheels, the whimsically named "Pit Stop" deodorant, and a mix for the spicy chili popular in his native East Texas. But ever the car-lover, he answered the call when his friend Lee Iacocca left Ford to take over at Chrysler in 1978, devising high-performance limited-edition Dodges in the 1980s at what finally became the Chrysler-Shelby Performance Center in Southern California. In 1990, at age 67, Shelby underwent a heart transplant, but returned to drive the Viper that paced the 1991 Indy 500—and to work on a new open-wheel V-6 "spec-racer" for SCCA, the Shelby Can Am.

As you'd expect, Shelby loves the new Dodge inspired by his Cobras. The Viper, he said, is "a beautiful car. I think it's reminiscent of the 1960s. It has the smooth, contoured lines of the Cobra. It handles very well. It doesn't have a lot of garbage hung on it. I'm very happy with the way it compares in performance."

CHAPTER THREE

Let's Build a Sports Car

It began one day in February 1988 with a brief discussion between Chrysler President Robert A. Lutz and Tom Gale, chief of design.

"I was walking down the hall, Bob called me in the office—and it was just a five-minute discussion," said Gale. "I can remember it like it was yesterday. He said,'I've been thinking more and more. We really ought to kick off doing a project like a reborn Cobra.' That was our intent right from the very beginning."

What Lutz had in mind was a sports car with a modern engine management system, new-think transmission, computer-aided suspension design, and world-class tires. The Viper would take advantage of the latest in modern technology. But it would not be a gadget-laden, high-tech wonder bristling with turbochargers, anti-lock brakes, four-wheel steering, adjustable shock-absorber damping, and all-wheel drive. Instead, the Viper would take a mechanically pure approach—loads of power fed to simple rear drive. Brute force. As in the Shelby Cobra, there would exist an unfiltered communication between driver, car, and road.

Lutz and Gale had such cars in their blood. Lutz, a former Marine jet-fighter pilot, is a passionate auto enthusiast and an accomplished driver. In his personal garage are a Brian Angliss Mark IV Autokraft Cobra 427 replica and several motorcycles. Gale, vice president of design, is a committed hot rodder who drives a 1970 Plymouth 'Cuda AAR.

However casual the pair's conversation may have been on the surface, several influences came together during those five minutes. One was centered around a concept vehicle designed by Chrysler's Pacifica design studio. The stylists had been exploring the packaging of a V-8 convertible sports car. Around 1985, the idea came together and a static concept vehicle called the Izod was produced.

"It would be wrong to say that Izod was done knowing that Viper was coming," explained Gale. "But when you take a look at the packaging, when you take a look at the overall vehicle pro-portion . . . you start to see the lineage in the vehicle . . . . one thing influences the other."

Another influence was a late-'80s engine development program. Lutz was one of the executives overseeing the truck division at Chrysler during this time and he craved a new stump-puller gasoline engine that would boost Dodge's image with big-pickup buyers.

A man who would prove vital to Viper, Francois Castaing, was at that time head of Chrysler's Jeep and Truck Engineering division. He had come over in July 1987, after a career in European motorsports, where he helped turbocharge Formula 1 as technical director of Renault's Formula 1 effort.

"One of the first major projects we got going was to put a new big V-10, a big gas truck engine, on its way," Castaing recalled. "Jokingly, we said, 'That's the kind of engine that back in the '60s, Bizzarrini and DeTomaso would have bought to create the great sports car of back then. You know,

Izod (*top two photos*), a 1985 design exercise, provided some conceptual groundwork when Chrysler laid out the original Viper styling themes (*bottom photos*) in early 1988.

30

very powerful, torquey, big gas American engine, put into a nice body.' And we kept saying, 'Well, maybe we should sell the engine to people like that.' Bob [Lutz] owns a Cobra, so Cobra was another car we talked about. One day—and I don't remember how it happened—but the idea of creating a concept car like the Cobra, using the big gas truck engine as a core, came up."

"It occurred to me," Lutz explained, "that Chrysler had all the bits and pieces in the parts bin. Whether it's the truck bin or the car bin, who cares? But we had all the pieces in the bin to do a show car that would pick up on the theme of the Cobra."

Using the brash Cobra as a touchstone brought to the forefront another irreplaceable influence: Carroll Shelby. Shelby had hooked up with Chrysler as a "performance consultant" in 1982, and by 1986, Shelby Automobiles Inc. was turning out hot, limited-edition Dodges. Shelby said that at the time Lutz approached him, he was in fact building a sports car of his own and trying to interest Chrysler in it. But along came Lutz and Castaing. Shelby recalled Lutz's

proposal: "'Why don't we build a sports car, something like the old 427 Cobra, only let's build a 1990s version of it—and what did I think of the idea?' We sat down about 30 minutes and conceptualized the car. He wanted to do what I'd been trying to get done around the company for nine years. In 30 minutes we had the concept . . . . And we ended up

Viper debuted at the 1989 Detroit Auto Show, and was a smash hit (*opposite page*). Tom Gale (*from left*), Carroll Shelby, Francois Castaing, and Bob Lutz—the car's "four fathers"—pose proudly with it. *Top*: Early show car version had conventional mirrors and lacked the targa bar of finished concept vehicle (*above*).

with the Viper, where it might have been years before we would have gotten management to agree to build what I was building."

Around that time Shelby was awaiting a heart transplant and therefore didn't have a direct hand in Viper's engineering or design. But the fathers of the Viper regard him as the "conscience" of the car, a voice that kept it true to the ethic of power and simplicity.

Just three weeks after Gale and Lutz had their five-minute talk, Gale was in Lutz's office discussing another topic. As their meeting was breaking up, Gale brought up the Viper project: "I said, 'I've got something else I want to run by you.' By then what we had was a few sketches, a full-size side view package, and a rendering of what we wanted to do with the car. And I said, 'This goes back to the discussion we had a few weeks ago, and I wanted to see what you think of it.' And he was really excited. I think more than anything, though, he was frankly surprised that we just took off and started to go."

These renderings were the product of Chrysler's Highland Park Advanced Design department. They show an open two-seater with a voluptuously wide body and the classic sports car long-nose, short-deck proportions. The trailing edges of the front fenders were open in the manner of race-car air extractors. The windshield was low and swept, with rearview mirrors that were integrated at its edges. A targa-type roll bar supported the head restraints. Full wheel openings stretched over enormous tires on rims with canyon-deep offsets.

In just three weeks, these drawings were transformed into a full-size clay model. Lutz approved, and on May 28, 1988, construction began on a two-seat sports-car concept for the 1989 auto-show circuit.

The show car's steel body was remarkably similar to the form that had been established in ink and clay, but the show car added an even more intimidating touch. Most of the original drawings showed exhaust tips exiting the lower rear fascia, and the clay model had coves below the doors that hinted at exhaust outlets. However, the show car did more than hint: Mushrooming from the caverns behind its front wheels were snake pits of exhaust headers. They gathered in the rocker panels and muscled under the doors as bona fide side exhausts, thick and threatening.

"I was a little shocked when I saw the first Viper workout," Lutz said. "It was to me more of a departure from the Cobra styling themes that I had personally envisaged. I would have done a more literal update of the Cobra. Obviously, you know, with a much faster windshield, but I probably would have had a tendency to keep the Cobra mouth and everything—which would have been wrong. Because then it would have been merely a restyle of the Cobra, whereas the Viper now is a totally unique car which is reminiscent in character of what a Cobra was. But it now stands unique, as opposed to being 'son of Cobra.'"

An automobile this impressive deserved something equally distinctive beneath the hood. And that was the V-10.

"We packaged the car around the V-10," Gale said. "One of the great justifications for this program was, 'Hey, why don't we take one of those engines and try just really making something special out of it, something that would really showcase what we had done.' The big question was, could we get a V-10? I couldn't get my hands on one. So when we built the concept car, we took a 360 (cubic-inch V-8) and literally grafted on the front two cylinders and made a running engine . . . So that's how those get done . . .

The show car's cockpit was all-business. Access to the pedals would be improved for production, but the basic design—*sans* wraparound mirrors—would survive with only minor alterations.

For the show car, a V-8 was turned into a V-10 (*above*) and foreshadowed the production engine. Flamboyant side exhaust system became another show-car signature, but would be modified for the customer versions.

lots of sweat and lots of good hard work behind the scenes." There would, of course, be more development work on the engine, but from the original concept the V-10 was linked to the Viper.

A name would be the final touch.

"I think I came up with it on an airplane trip," Lutz said. "What it was is, you wanted the snake and we couldn't have 'Cobra.' It was as simple as that. You didn't want 'Sidewinder' because it had military connotations and, secondly, you could see all kinds of buff-book headlines with the car going sideways. 'Asp' doesn't sound too good. 'Python'—they're big and fat and they swallow pigs and then lie around in the sun for a week. So 'Viper' seemed to be . . . It rolls off of the tongue easily. And the only resistance we got to Viper was some of the marketing guys, with the show car, wanted to call it Dodge Challenger, I think."

Painted a gleaming red, the Dodge Viper RT/10 debuted on January 4, 1989, at the North American International Auto Show in Detroit. It was a sensation.

Showgoers crowded 12-deep to get a glimpse. It was the feature

story in enthusiast magazines. Photos of it appeared in daily newspapers. Chrysler received hundreds of letters from the public, begging that Viper be put into production. Some admirers even sent deposit checks—which were returned. Lutz was quoted as saying a high-ranking friend at Ford had contacted him about obtaining one. It was a brilliant, satisfying moment.

"And now we're together at the show, and the car is really attracting a lot of attention," recalled Castaing. "And I remember we were all together being photographed on the display—Carroll Shelby, Bob, and myself. And I remember us saying, Now that everybody wants the

car, what are we going to do to make one?"

A week after the Detroit unveiling, Chrysler Corporation Chairman Lee Iacocca said his company would decide Viper's fate in the second quarter of 1990. On May 18, 1990, Chrysler announced that it would build the Viper for sale in limited numbers.

The story was only beginning.

A one-of-a-kind plastic-bodied sports car wows auto-show crowds, people start waving checks, and the maker starts thinking of selling copies. That's the story of the first Chevrolet Corvette in January 1953 and the Dodge Viper concept car of January 1989.

Both these dream machines were conceived not merely for publicity, but designed as a means of drawing attention to exciting new passenger models that were just around the corner. Both would move rapidly into production largely unchanged, thanks to enthusiastic public response and support from top executives with the clout to make show cars into "real" cars.

As well, Viper would be just as significant to Chrysler as the original 'Vette was to General Motors, with a purpose far beyond that of "image car." It

would be nothing less than a multi-faceted experiment—a ground-up, rolling testbed for a company then starting a ground-up transformation.

Despite the concept Viper's overwhelmingly positive reception, the decision to proceed with a showroom version came neither quickly nor easily. Initial thoughts were to contract engineering and production to ASC, Inc., the well-known Michigan-based specialist builder of low-volume cars. Another prospect was Carroll Shelby's small shop in Southern California, then turning out special performance-tuned Dodge Lancers and Shadows.

But inevitably, as Francois Castaing recalled, "The idea of making the car [ourselves] grew rapidly." He helped it along when he made this argument to Chrysler president Bob Lutz: "I said to him that we can look at Viper as just a car, or as a technical exercise, a challenge. If it is a technical exercise, we could justify the full burden on the

Chrysler drew men and women from a multitude of disciplines to form Team Viper. Some members pose here around the car and Roy Sjoberg, chief Viper engineer.

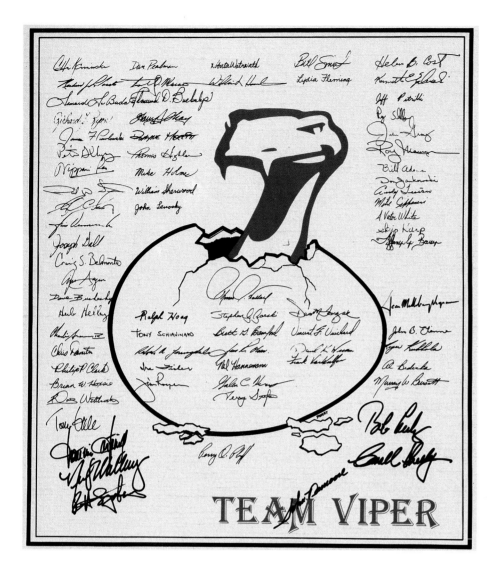

TEAM VIPER

formation of Team Viper to study the feasibility of building "Bob Lutz's Cobra." To head the group, Castaing selected Roy H. Sjoberg, a thoughtful, personable veteran engineer who had come to Highland Park in early 1985 after 25 years with GM. While working for the world's largest automaker, Sjoberg participated in numerous "skunkworks" projects—including the several mid-engine Corvette experimentals of the early and mid-'70s.

From more than 200 Chrysler employees who volunteered for Team Viper, Sjoberg chose about 20 self-proclaimed car nuts from departments such as design, engineering, manufacturing, and procurement and supply. Their immediate task was to determine how quickly Viper could be built and at what cost.

But Team Viper had another task of larger, longer-range importance: testing an entirely new approach to building cars— one that Chrysler was already moving to. Called the "Team Concept," it brings the above-mentioned disciplines together in a group dedicated to a single product or platform. The idea revolves around cutting costs, lead

A "team" approach created Chrysler's minivans in the 1980s. But for Viper, the concept was applied to a faster development schedule and included outside suppliers. It also was a testbed for the vital 1993 LH sedan effort, and demanded such dedication that its members came to think of themselves as the "Viper family." Their signatures on this placard symbolize their pride in "hatching" an important car.

company, and also use it as a training ground for our engineers. One of my personal objectives when I took overall responsibility for Chrysler Engineering was to reestablish its reputation," which Castaing admits had been tarnished by too many years with too many variants on the capable but humble front-wheel-drive K-car compact.

Thus, on March 28, 1989, just 12 weeks after the concept Viper's smash debut, Chrysler management approved the

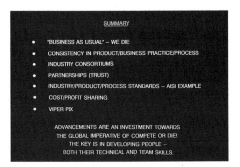

times, and mistakes by having all required specialists work side-by-side from a car platform's very beginning. This is in contrast to traditional Detroit practice where a project passes from Design to Engineering to Manufacturing and so on, with little communication except when problems arise—in which case the project gets passed back "up the line" and then down again.

Also early on, a Viper Technical Policy Committee (TPC) was formed, with the concept car's "four fathers" as its nucleus: Lutz, Engineering Vice-President Castaing, Product Design chief Tom Gale, and performance consultant Carroll Shelby. Team Viper would have total responsibility for the production model, but would meet with the TPC every three months or so to report progress and review program direction.

Moving this type of streamlined decision-making down the ranks was unheard-of at Chrysler or any other Detroit automaker. But it was nothing compared to the ambitious goals Team Viper set for itself. Within three months, Sjoberg and company reported to the TPC that they could not only

deliver a road-ready Viper, but could do so in just three years and for only $50 million—a pittance even for then-struggling Chrysler, and an incredibly low sum for the development of an all-new car, which usually runs into billions.

"My ulterior motive," Sjoberg said later, "was to be so cheap that everyone would leave us alone—to set such impossible tasks that bureaucracy, which would normally get in the way, would say 'I'm not gonna go *near* that.' And they *did* stay away—until they realized this thing was going to be a success. Then we got more bureaucracy than we wanted. They would say we could not do something because it was against corporate procedure. Well, I had the advantage of Bob Lutz. He gave us only two charters: be ethical and be moral—and don't worry about the procedure manual."

Slides from a talk on Computer Aided Engineering that Sjoberg made before a software supplier are a primer on the Viper doctrine, including "Keep it Simple," and "'Business as Usual'—We Die."

Team members at the New Mack plant. In top-left photo are (*from left*) James Royer, engine manager; Howard Lewis, plant manager; Herb Helbig, vehicle synthesis manager; Ken O'Donnell, production control manager; Roy Sjoberg, chief engineer; William Smith, manufacturing manager. Bottom right: Helbig with two Viper craftspersons.

There was plenty else to worry about anyway, not the least of which was turning an impractical showmobile into a legal, practical road machine. "Everybody loved the concept car," Sjoberg said, "but it had a foundry-brazed V-8 with two more cylinders on it, had no legal bumper systems or vision requirements. I couldn't get my foot off the accelerator to hit the brake pedal because the instrument panel was in the way. There were a lot of non-feasible issues. So we really redesigned the concept car, but never changed the appearance. I think that's a key success of the Team: taking

something that was not feasible—that had no feasibility studies, no *drawings*—and making a feasible product out of it, to where you put the two side-by-side and can't really tell the difference." Herb Helbig, Team Viper's Vehicle Synthesis Manager, put the matter more bluntly: "Pure and simple, we had to turn a fairy tale into real life."

Several key early decisions remained true to the concept-car fable while speeding it to reality. Viper would be a strictly limited-production item, with no high-tech features to add cost, complexity, and delay. Said Castaing: "We wanted no unnecessary technology, no useless gimmicks, nothing to detract from driving satisfaction or the owner's responsibility for driving the machine." Likewise,

there would be no options, nor even expected features like roll-up windows or automatic transmission. "The real secret was keeping the program small and the car simple," said Lutz. "Had the traditional planning people gotten involved, the program risked growing to huge proportions. So we gave the responsibility to the Team and told them your investment *is* and your piece-cost target *is,* and you are not to say yes to anything that risks violating those targets—because the minute they are, the program stops. And that gave Roy the power to say no."

"There was also an initial shock," explained Lutz. "Guys would say, 'In my past I've done this little piece of the steering system, but you mean now I'm responsible for the *whole* system?'

And we'd say, 'Right!' It was the realization that the group in this room would have to do the whole car."

Low weight was a high priority, especially for Cobramaster Shelby. Though health problems prevented Shelby from attending all meetings of the Technical Policy Committee, Castaing said that the Texan kept "bugging the Team about weight all the time." Observed Lutz: "Carroll was the spiritual conscience of the car, to make sure that nobody forgot what it was supposed to be. Francois was there to offer a *lot* of good technical guidance. With his Formula 1 background, he was a terrific motivator to the Team. I was making sure it was also going

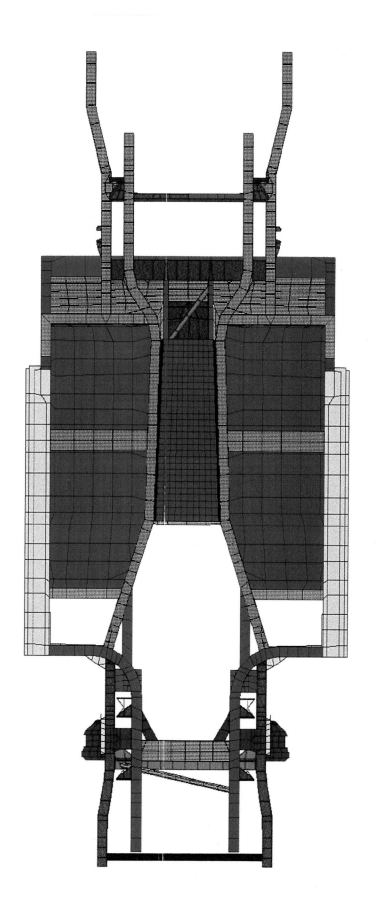

to be a good business proposition, and Tom Gale was there to protect the aesthetic integrity of the car."

Gale also praised Castaing's efforts: "He was the one who ultimately had to set aside the resources and say, 'We're gonna *do* this. Otherwise, it could have died a thousand deaths." Castaing himself was modest: "Most of the time we [on the TPC] let the team find the 'how' to do a thing, but at some points we decided what the 'what' was going to be."

Though the concept Viper's basic looks and V-10 powerplant were never seriously debated, the cast-iron engine being developed for Dodge's forthcoming T300 full-size pickup was deemed too heavy and created handling problems. Weight concerns also prompted the use of a steel-tube space-frame *monocoque,* or "birdcage," instead of an orthodox platform chassis. This brought the added advantages of reduced cost and somewhat easier manufacturing. Still, Castaing observed, Chrysler had to "learn" about building a space-frame, as it had little production experience with such structures.

Experience, not weight, also

prompted the decision to render most of the production exterior body panels by the new resin transfer molding process (RTM) instead of in steel, as on the show car. Indeed, Castaing said he chose Sjoberg as chief project engineer partly because of his GM experience with "plastic" bodies. Chrysler was aware that impending competitive products like the subcompact Saturn and GM200 minivans would use

It may evoke a retro feel, but Viper itself is not "low tech." For example, computers helped design its notably rigid frame and ferret out suspension stress points.

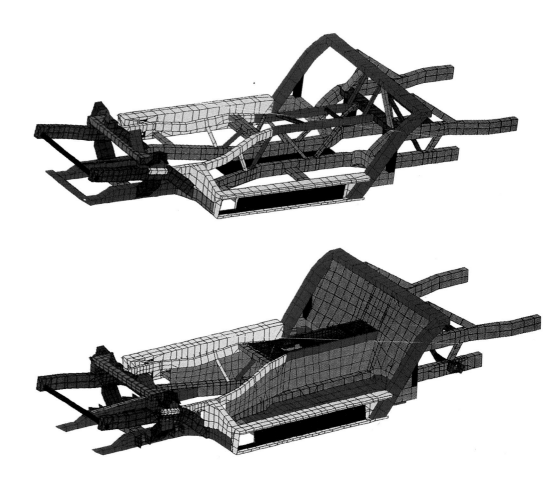

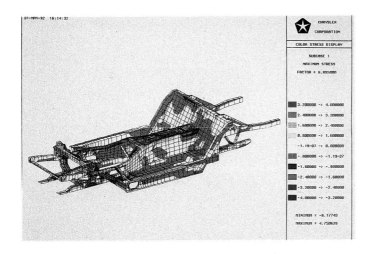

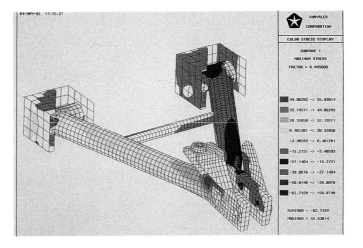

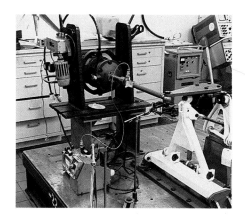

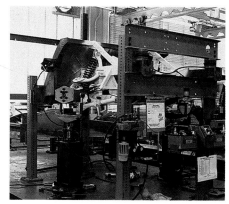

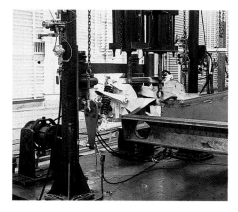

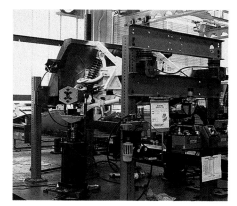

One secret to streamlining Viper's development and construction was to have suppliers ship major components as pre-assembled units. Here the suspension, which utilizes Koni shock absorbers, undergoes testing.

panels of plastic-like composites. Chrysler planned to use similar panels on its own future models, including the critical 1993 "LH" mid-size sedans. The company's desire to "catch up" on such new materials explains why aluminum was never even considered for the production Viper body.

Though Team Viper and the TPC watched weight throughout the program, they willingly compromised when paring

pounds threatened to increase cost, complexity, or time. As Castaing admitted: "We missed the weight target. Several times along the way we realized that we had to either increase the cost of some of the parts, to make them lighter, or take more time to test different solutions. But we were not too concerned, because the engine turned out much more powerful and torquey than we realized."

To help make it so—and save

both time and weight—Castaing put in a call to Mauro Forghieri at Lamborghini Engineering, the technology and Formula 1 development arm of Chrysler's legendary Italian sports-car subsidiary. Lamborghini joined the Viper project in May 1989, at which point Chrysler hadn't even built a cast-iron truck V-10. So Highland Park sent a cadre of engineers to Italy with only drawings in hand. "We knew the Team was working at least 18 months ahead of the truck engine," Castaing recalled. "So I said 'let's modify [the truck V-10] the way we feel we want to have it [for the Viper].' And we decided we wanted to go with aluminum, replace the [truck unit's] cast-iron block and head with aluminum. I suggested using Lamborghini's prototyping abilities and experience with aluminum to help us make the conversion and save time.

"The deal we had with Forghieri was that Lamborghini would help us redesign the block and head for aluminum conversion, and then cast parts for, say, 15 engines as fast as they could in their Formula 1 shops. They assembled the first two aluminum engines, to make sure all the parts and machining were okay, and then shipped everything back. We then took over completely. Everything else was done right here [in Detroit]."

Meanwhile, Team Viper was growing along with its workload—and struggling with the difficulties of working *as* a team. Cleverness was one order of those days. Sjoberg recounted how the group "found" its home in the old Jeep/Truck Engineering

Spies snapped the V-8 Viper prototype and mistook the new Viper logo for the Eagle brand emblem (*top two photos*). Work on the V-10 engine, a mockup of which is pictured at far right, was well underway at the time. At right: the six-speed transmission.

45

Dodge teased auto writers in June 1990 with the first V-10 Viper prototype. Unlike the V-8 mule, it had side exhausts, but they were enveloped by the rocker panels. Neither the chrome wheels nor the hood tie-down pins would see production.

(JTE) building on Plymouth Road in Detroit: "We were working primarily out of a warehouse the first couple of weeks, when one of our mechanics noticed that the Jeep design staff was moving out of its area at JTE. I called Trevor Creed [Chrysler's Interior Design chief] and asked if it was true. He told me to keep it quiet because no one knew they were moving to Highland Park. They say

possession is nine-tenths of the law, so we moved in . . . that night. We haven't moved since."

Inventiveness became policy. Unused equipment often ended up in Team Viper's hands, everything from hoists to hotplates. "We didn't steal anything from other groups," Sjoberg said. "We just used good intelligence to find out when equipment was being under-

utilized, then asked if we could borrow it. We did a lot of good old-fashioned horse-trading to get some of our tools."

A far greater challenge, Sjoberg felt, was "starting to tear the [professional] walls down and talk to each other." Getting comfortable took time. As Sjoberg recalled: "When we started, a lot of people had their desks facing a wall in an open room. And it was just about three months when my secretary said, 'Did you notice what happened today? The last desk turned around'—so we were all looking into the room at each other. Later, we had the chance to have offices again, but everyone

voted not to create offices with closeable doors." Meanwhile, the Team had created a detailed, 36-month timeline covering over 900 critical events—everything from moving in, up to, and beyond Production Job 1.

Time was of the essence, as was speed. By late August, a suspension development "mule" powered by a Chrysler 360-cubic-inch (5.9-liter) V-8 was under test. By fall, Team Viper had adapted the concept-car shape into producible, fully legal form without changing its essential appearance.

In December 1989, just 11 months after the show car's

debut, a Viper prototype was spotted by spy photographers near Chrysler's Kingman, Arizona, proving grounds, accompanied by a new Corvette roadster and a Shelby Cobra. Painted white, the Viper sported a full roll cage instead of the concept car's hooped "sportbar," and lacked its side pipes and exposed headers (an under-car exhaust system was

Early reports put Viper's V-10 at 7.0 liters, but even the development engine (*below*) displaced the full 8.0 liters of the production unit. The cabin was moving toward final form in materials and design.

devised to make it road-legal). But the car did sport the new Viper logo, which some journalists mistook for the badge of Chrysler's Eagle brand, leading to talk that the "Cobra for the '90s" wouldn't be a Dodge at all. The interior was a rough version of the concept Viper's, while the 17-inch road wheels were attractive custom affairs dissimilar to both the show car's and the eventual production design. Tire sizes, though, would not change: 275/40 front, 335/35 rear.

A V-10 still wasn't ready, so the white mule carried another 360 V-8, this time tuned for about 300 horsepower and mated to a six-speed manual gearbox from Getrag of Germany. This led to rumors that a similar V-8 would be standard, with the V-10 (then rumored to displace 7.0 liters) an option. Lutz, who drove this mule (as did Castaing), later said it "wasn't a bad car. We would not have been ashamed to also have had a V-8 in the program."

Indeed, some letter-writers, and a few company hands, had argued for a revival of Chrysler's famed 425-cid Hemi V-8. But Castaing was against it: "I didn't believe it made a lot of sense to

reproduce a legend. On top of that, Bob and Tom and I strongly felt that the V-10 was part of the car's mystique." Goodbye, V-8.

Finally, a V-10 prototype was up and running in mid-April 1990. A month later, in Los Angeles, chairman Lee Iacocca ended his flag-waving, coast-to-coast "Chrysler in the '90s" whistle-stop tour by announcing that the Viper would indeed be built for sale, starting with model-year 1992.

Viper's original design had the headlamps located within the hood itself, as on this prototype. But the lights vibrated so much that they were anchored to the front fascia for production.

Chrysler itself released photos of the V-10 car, and even gave rides to selected automotive journalists. This prototype was much cleaner than the V-8 mules: painted red (as would all production '92s) and again showing the targa-type sportbar and side exhaust pipes. The concept car's road lamps were absent, but racing-style hood tiedowns were new (though not destined to survive).

With Iacocca's announcement, Team Viper moved full bore toward its self-imposed Job 1 deadline. Personnel expanded from about 60 to 85 as finance, manufacturing, and purchasing experts came aboard. Chrysler's Mack Avenue facility in downtown Detroit was chosen as the production site, and renamed the New Mack Avenue Viper Assembly Plant. There the car would go together in "old-world" fashion—and with an unusually high number of supplied sub-assemblies (including the entire frame)—on just 300 feet of conveyor line (versus several miles in many auto factories). Ultimately, some 120-160 workers were recruited under a historic five-year agreement with the United Auto Workers union that made "craftsperson" the one and only job classification at New Mack. The pact also made each craftsperson responsible for verifying quality and even securing materials, which meant delegating more authority to lower-echelon workers. All craftspersons were considered members of Team Viper and, not surprisingly, were organized into small groups, each with its own elected leader.

Suppliers also became part of the Team, including several with no prior auto-industry experience. Some vendors thought the project too small or too alien at first, but

most were ultimately infected by the Team's enthusiasm for both its mission and its machine. "They understood that we were willing to take risks and to work with them," observed Synthesis Manager Herb Helbig, "but they weren't used to that. And in fact, they approached it cautiously until they could work with the Team a while. Then they got caught up in the euphoria. And all of a sudden, they started to do things they didn't think they could do, or weren't willing to try or were afraid to try, because they learned that's the normal course of doing business here. A great many of our suppliers even developed

Viper teams within their own organizations." Other suppliers sent representatives to take up residence at Team headquarters.

One result of all these chummy new relationships was the adoption of numerous supplier suggestions that improved product quality, simplified manufacturing, and saved time and money. An example is Viper's patented one-piece windshield frame–dashtop, an idea from Rockwell International.

Many vendors went out of their way for Viper's sake. Kelsey-Hayes, for instance, advanced the timetable for its new "modular full-face" wheels so Viper could have them first. Borg-Warner put the rush on a new six-speed gearbox when Getrag became unable to supply transmissions halfway through the program.

That program, according to Castaing, was planned all along as a "pay-as-you-go" effort in three

phases, with Job 1 capping Phase I. That came on December 9, 1991, when the first full assembly-line model rolled out of New Mack—and was promptly given to Chairman Lee Iacocca. The production Viper was formally unveiled the following month, again at Detroit. It was precisely three years after the concept car appeared. Chrysler had delivered its dream: on time, on budget, as promised.

But the mission was far from accomplished. Job 1 also began Phase II, which called for some 200 Vipers built as 1992 models with temporary tooling. Phase III would commence with 1993-model production: an anticipated build of 2000-3000 with final tooling.

For the benefit of future historians, the first six production Vipers were sent out (in special unmarked trucks) on May 20, 1992, about two months later than planned. Cerritos Dodge in

Chrysler ran Viper prototypes for thousands of miles at its Michigan and Arizona proving grounds, and on city streets, open highways, mountain roads, and road race courses across the U.S. By June 1991, the interior was production ready.

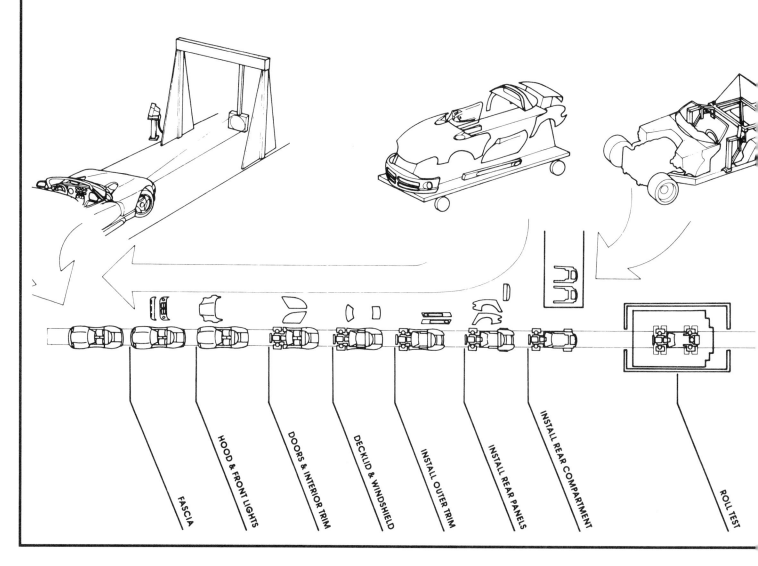

FASCIA

HOOD & FRONT LIGHTS

DOORS & INTERIOR TRIM

DECKLID & WINDSHIELD

INSTALL OUTER TRIM

INSTALL REAR PANELS

INSTALL REAR COMPARTMENT

ROLL TEST

Southern California, the nation's top-selling Dodge dealer, received the lowest serial number, 18. The first 17 examples were retained by Chrysler. Of these, four were earmarked for press use, two for show duty (including Iacocca's Number-1), and the remainder for internal engineering and quality evaluations. Perhaps the ultimate pre-production Viper is the 1991 Indy 500 pace car driven by none

other than Carroll Shelby (see Chapter 5).

Though its story is just beginning, Viper has already made history, has already become a legend. As Bob Lutz observed,

"This car has an importance to Chrysler that goes way beyond its numbers or the size of its investment. In fact, it's done things for the whole perception of the U.S. automobile industry

CHASSIS ASSEMBLY

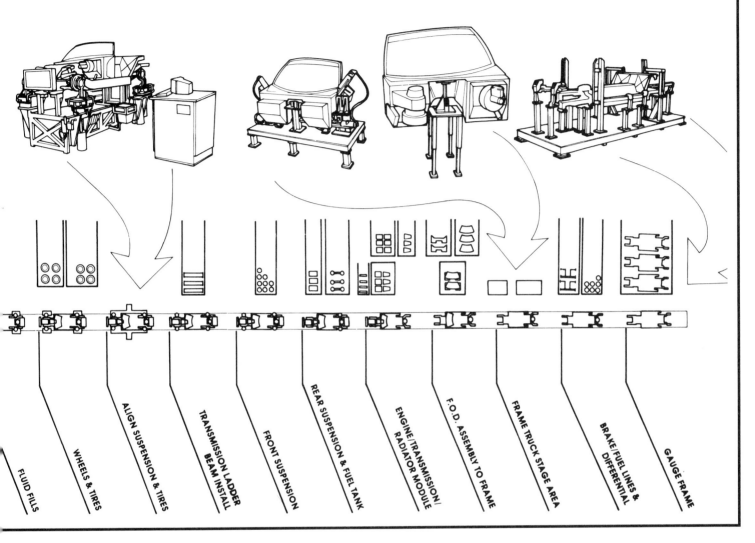

FLUID FILLS

WHEELS & TIRES

ALIGN SUSPENSION & TIRES

TRANSMISSION LADDER BEAM INSTALL

FRONT SUSPENSION

REAR SUSPENSION & FUEL TANK

ENGINE/TRANSMISSION/RADIATOR MODULE

F.O.D. ASSEMBLY TO FRAME

FRAME TRUCK STAGE AREA

BRAKE/FUEL LINES & DIFFERENTIAL

GAUGE FRAME

versus Japan . . . The fact that we were able to do it with a small team, do it quickly and for very little money, just speaks volumes about the transformation of Chrysler."

And for the future of Chrysler and maybe all of Detroit. Quite an achievement for one car, even a "modern Cobra."

Viper assembly is depicted here, running right to left. Body panels go on the car from the rear forward and chassis work is done without body parts attached, to reduce damage to the skin.

With "fathers" like Cobra-owner Bob Lutz and Cobra-originator Carroll Shelby, it's hardly a wonder that the Viper hews so closely to the concept of its great '60s forebearer. In many ways Viper is a technical cousin to the hallowed Shelby Cobra. The difference is that Chrysler's snake meets government regulations no Cobra ever faced:

everything from headlamp height to exhaust emissions.

Despite these regulations, the Viper is, like the Cobra, a true roadster. The lack of roll-up windows, seating for two, and an orthodox front-engine/rear-drive format complete the resemblance. Both are built around light-but-strong multi-tube "space-frames"

and ride classic all-independent suspensions with double wishbones and coil springs at each corner, strengthened with anti-roll bars front and rear. Rack-and-pinion steering and big all-disc brakes are also common to both cars. So, too, are cast wheels wearing the biggest tires the bodywork can contain.

But the similarities end there. Not counting appearance, Viper's most obvious departure is its driveline. Instead of a 7.0-liter (427-cubic-inch) V-8, there's an 8.0-liter (488-cid) V-10—Chrysler's largest-ever passenger-car engine. As noted in Chapter 3, it's based on the V-10 originally designed for Dodge's 1994 T300 truck line, but its block and heads are cast in weight-saving aluminum, rather than iron. Though engineers pared 100 pounds from the truck unit's weight, the Viper version still flattens the scales at 716 pounds.

Viper is 3.4 inches shorter than a Corvette, but it's 2.6 wider than the Chevy and 2.3 inches wider, in fact, than a Cadillac Sedan de Ville!

It's bulky as well. This is due in part to a 90-degree cylinder bank angle (as in a V-8), rather than the 72 degrees desirable for even firing pulses in a V-10. Still, the crankshaft—forged steel, of course—has throws arranged for 72 degrees. This gives close to even-firing without split throws. It also gives a rather lumpy idle.

Like most '90s performance engines, this V-10 is fed by sequential multiport fuel injection with integrated electronic ignition. It breathes through two sets of tuned intake runners—here, five-branch affairs, each with a plenum connected to a throttle body. Valvegear apes the Cobra's and is strictly passé: two valves per cylinder actuated by pushrods and rocker arms controlled by a single camshaft in the valley of the engine "vee." However, hydraulic roller lifters are a modern touch.

Engine Manager Jim Royer said such relative simplicity reflects the Viper's fast-track development schedule. "Because of time constraints . . . we took a straightforward approach. We didn't want to risk getting into exotic technology in so short a span."

But several features are at least semi-exotic. One is an external coolant manifold alongside the block, an idea from Lamborghini Engineering in Italy. A supplement to normal water-jacketing and inspired by Formula 1 practice, this arrangement saved 20 pounds and a critical 3/4-inch in topside length (needed to clear the hoodline). It also permitted, as Royer noted, "individually tuned cooling for each head and cylinder liner" (the latter made of iron, as is usual in aluminum-block engines). The result, explained Royer, is "very good cooling" with "probably the lowest water temperature rise of any engine Chrysler has ever built."

Also reducing engine height is Chrysler's first use of bottom-feed fuel injectors, though they were chosen mainly for cost reasons. Chrysler planned to use the fuel injectors in future high-volume engines, so the engine, as in so many other areas, became a small-scale testbed for new technology. Royer says the chief advantages of bottom-feeders are that they have a lower tendency to trap fuel vapor, which means better driveability, and they also run cooler than top-feed squirters. And in Viper's case, they allowed the fuel rail to be cast as an integral part of the intake manifolding.

Viper's fuel injection employs two "black boxes" instead of the usual one, both supplied by Chrysler's Huntsville, Alabama, electronics operation; and unlike many modern FI systems, this one has no knock sensors. Said Royer: "Again, to make a relatively simple engine, we just backed off on the compression ratio [which is set at 9:1] to have an adequate margin with the premium no-lead fuels that are available. In fact, we can run with *regular* no-lead most of the time." Equally impressive, Viper's V-10 meets all near-term

emissions levels without exhaust-gas recirculation.

Such thorough engineering gives the Viper powerplant the lowest height of any 90-degree "vee" engine in Chrysler history—25.9 inches from the oil-pan bottom to the uppermost brackets. It's also among the most potent of Chrysler engines. Rated horsepower is a bountiful 400 at 4600 rpm. Peak torque measures 450 pounds/feet at 3600, though some 400 lbs/ft is available from as little as 1200 rpm (which, by the way, is about three times normal idle speed).

Putting this muscle to the ground is a new six-speed Borg-Warner manual transmission. Though first devised for a non-Chrysler 1993 model, its timetable was advanced for Viper's early-1992 introduction and given a beefier geartrain with new ratios to match the V-10's power and torque curves. Like the six-speed Getrag unit in recent Corvettes,

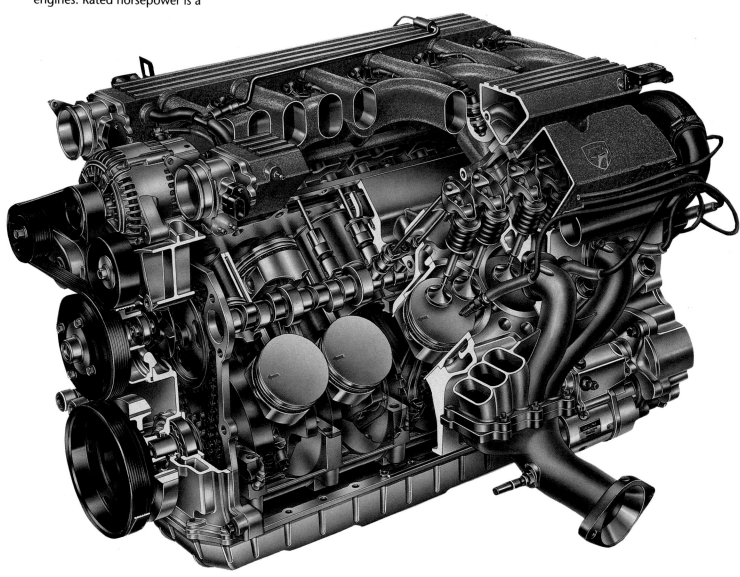

this B-W features a "forced" 1-4 computer-mandated upshift at light throttle openings as a fuel economy measure. Also like the Getrag, the top two ratios are rangy overdrives (0.74:1 and 0.50:1). The high sixth gear contributes to Viper's top speed of more than 160 mph.

Because space is tight in its body/chassis package, Viper employs dual metal-monolithic catalytic converters, about 40 percent smaller than ordinary types. Limited space also complicated heat dissipation from an engine and exhaust system that can reach temperatures up to 1000

Viper's aluminum 488-cid V-10 is Chrysler's biggest engine ever. Conceived as a cast-iron truck motor and tailored for Viper duty by Lamborghini, it uses proven overhead valves (two per cylinder), but has innovative bottom-fed fuel injection.

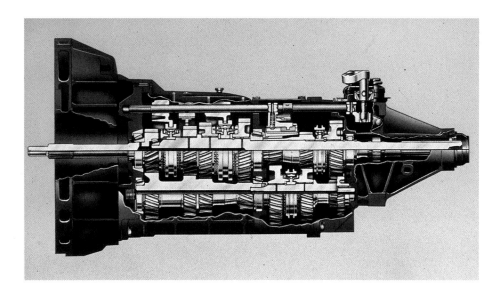

degrees, so Team Viper turned to Nomex—but as "pressed spaceboard" borrowed from the aerospace field, not the fiber familiar in burn-resistant driver's suits. This board appears as a 3mm "filler" within the aluminum "sandwich" of the lower rocker skins that surround the exposed side pipes. Small holes in the bottom of the sills also aid cooling. Containing interior heat buildup is a mat of thermal aluminum foil beneath the carpeting. Similar foil wraps around the exhaust manifolds.

It was under the hood that another space squeeze precluded a single motor for the windshield wipers, which were designed for a synchronized cross-over sweep.

The solution was a pair of small motors linked electronically. These are actually rear-wiper units from Chrysler's minivans.

Like the gearbox, Viper's distinctive tri-spoke wheels were brought out sooner than planned. Supplied by the Western Wheel Division of Kelsey-Hayes, which calls their design "modular full-face," they comprise a load-bearing outer section of cast aluminum welded to a lighter, spun-aluminum inner whose main function is tire sealing. Rim diameter is 17 inches all-round, with the fronts measuring 10 inches wide, and the rears a race-car-like 13.

Brakes are equally massive: 13 × 1.26 inches fore, 13 × 0.86-in. aft—all vented, of course. They come from Kelsey-Hayes's Italian Brembo operation that supplies Ferrari, Porsche, Lamborghini, and most of today's Formula 1 teams. Typical of Team Viper's "keep it

Six-speed Borg-Warner manual transmission "forces" a 1-4 upshift under light throttle.

simple" credo, K-H supplies complete wheel/brake assemblies ready to install.

"Plastic cars" are nothing new, but Viper is the first to employ the resin transfer molding process (RTM) for most exterior body panels. The lone exception is a lower body enclosure of sheet molding compound (SMC). With RTM, glass fibers are placed in a mold that is then closed and injected with resin. This produces stronger panels with less pressure and less labor than the more widely used SMC, in which a resin-impregnated fiberglass mat is cured under intense pressure. RTM requires only 10-15 minutes of hand-finishing for top-flight appearance, versus hours of handwork for SMC.

Cars like the BMW Z1 and Lotus Esprit also use RTM panels. But Team Viper wanted to better their finish quality while saving weight with panels only $1/10$-inch thick (versus the more manageable $1/8$-inch). This prompted development of a finish-quality test where light is beamed onto a surface at acute angles to reveal

(Continued on page 67)

COMPARATIVE SPECIFICATIONS:

Dodge Viper RT/10 vs. Chevrolet Corvette ZR-1 and Shelby Cobra 427SC			
GENERAL	**1992-93 Dodge Viper RT/10**	**1993 Chevrolet Corvette ZR-1**	**1965 Shelby Cobra 427SC**
Vehicle type	2-seat roadster	2-seat hatchback coupe	2-seat roadster
Drivetrain layout	Front engine/ rear drive	Front engine/ rear drive	Front engine/ rear drive
Construction	Tubular steel chassis with RTM body panels	Welded steel "uniframe" with fiberglass (SMC) body panels	Tubular steel chassis with aluminum body
Original base price	$50,000	$65,000	$7,495
Wheelbase (in.)	96.2	96.2	90.0
Overall length (in.)	175.1	178.5	156.0
Overall height (in.)	43.9	46.3	49.0
Overall width (in.)	75.7	73.1	70.0
Track, front/rear (in.)	59.6/60.6	57.7/60.6	56.0/56.0
Curb weight (lbs)	3400	3503	2660
Weight distribution, front/rear (%)	50.6/49.4[1]	52/48	46.6/53.4[1]
ENGINE			
Type	ohv V-10	dohc V-8	ohv V-8
Displacement (cc/ci)	7990/488	5736/350	7011/427
Bore × stroke (mm/in.)	101.6 x 98.5/ 4.00 x 3.88	99 x 93/ 3.90 x 3.66	107.4 x 96/ 4.23 x 3.78
Number valves	20	32	16
Compression ratio	9.1:1	11.0:1	10.5:1

ENGINE *(Continued)*	1992-93 Dodge Viper RT/10	1993 Chevrolet Corvette ZR-1	1965 Shelby Cobra 427SC
Fuel delivery	Chrysler sequential multiport; bottom- feed injectors	GM sequential multiport	1 x 4bbl Holley
Horsepower @ rpm	400 @ 4600	405 @ 5800	425 @ 6000[2]
Torque (lbs/ft) @ rpm	450 @ 3600	385 @ 4800	480 @ 3700[2]
Construction	aluminum heads and block	aluminum heads and block	cast-iron heads and block

TRANSMISSION

	1992-93 Dodge Viper RT/10	1993 Chevrolet Corvette ZR-1	1965 Shelby Cobra 427SC
Make/type	Borg-Warner 6-speed manual	ZF 6-speed manual	Ford 4-speed manual
Forward gear ratios (:1)	2.66/1.78/1.30/ 1.00/0.74/0.50	2.68/1.80/1.31/ 1.00/0.75/0.50	2.32/1.59/ 1.29/1.00
Final drive ratio (:1)	3.07	3.45	3.54/3.77/4.11
Differential	Hypoid type with limited slip	Hypoid type with limited slip	Hypoid type with limited slip

CHASSIS

	1992-93 Dodge Viper RT/10	1993 Chevrolet Corvette ZR-1	1965 Shelby Cobra 427SC
Suspension, front/rear	independent; unequal-length upper & lower control arms, coil-over-shock units, anti-roll bar/independent; unequal-length upper & lower control arms, toe link, coil-over- shock units, anti-roll bar (all shock absorbers gas charged)	independent; unequal-length upper & lower control arms, transverse monoleaf spring, anti-roll bar/ independent; five links with transverse monoleaf spring, tie-rods, anti-roll bar; "FX3" variable- rate shock absorbers	independent; unequal-length upper & lower control arms, coil springs, anti-roll bar/ independent; unequal-length upper & lower control arms, coil springs, anti-roll bar; hydraulic shock absorbers
Brakes, front/rear	13 x 1.26-in. vented discs/ 13 x 0.86-in. vented discs; hydraulic assist	13 x 1.10-in. vented discs/ 12 x 0.79-in. discs; vacuum assist; Bosch ABS II	11.6-in. discs/10.8-in. discs (by Girling)
Steering	Rack-and-pinion, power assist	Rack-and-pinion, power assist	Rack-and-pinion

CHASSIS (Continued)	1992-93 Dodge Viper RT/10	1993 Chevrolet Corvette ZR-1	1965 Shelby Cobra 427SC
Ratio (:1)	16.7	15.6	NA
Turns lock-to-lock	2.4	2.3	3.5
Turn diameter (ft)	40.7	40	36.0
Wheels, type	Cast-aluminum face welded to spun-alumimum rim	Cast alumimum	Halibrand cast magnesium
Size, front/rear (diameter x width, in.)	17 x 10.0/ 17 x 13.0	17 x 9.5/ 17 x 11.0	15 x 7.5/ 15 x 9.5
Tires	Michelin XGT-Z	Goodyear Eagle GS-C	Goodyear Blue Streak Sports Car Special
Size, front	P275/40ZR17	P275/40ZR17	6.00-15
rear	P335/35ZR17	P315/35ZR17	8.00-15
PERFORMANCE[1]			
Lbs/bhp	8.5	9.3	6.3[2]
Lbs/torque	7.6	9.4	5.5[2]
0-60 mph	4.4-4.6	4.9	4.1
0-100 mph	10.8-11.7	11.3	10.1
0-1/4 mi., sec. @ mph	13.1 @ 108	13.4 @ 109	12.6 @ 110
Observed top speed, mph	163	171	134
Braking, 70-0 mph, ft	180	159	NA
Skidpad acceleration, g	0.91	0.87	0.88

[1] *Car and Driver* March, July 1992; ZR-1 figures for 375-bhp 1992 model; Cobra figures for 4.11:1 final drive
[2] SAE gross; others: SAE net

Viper resurrects the muscle sports car, with few amenities to spoil the effect.

ZR-1 takes a high-tech approach: DOHC V-8, traction control, ABS, and adjustable suspension.

Cobra 427 is the quintessential big-block roadster. It has a wild, bare-knuckles character.

(Continued from page 62)

any flaws, which are then photographed and computer-analyzed. The reference standard is a sheet of fine plate glass— "flaw factor" 0. On a scale of 0-1000, Viper panels are claimed to score 150 or less.

Engineers also chose nickel-shell tooling for the panel molds, which not only costs less than conventional steel but shortens tooling changeover time. In fact, Chrysler says it can alter Viper's RTM panels on only one-year's notice.

Four more body features deserve mention. One is the combined windshield frame/dashtop, which Chrysler has patented. Suggested by supplier Rockwell International, it comprises a foam-wrapped steel core and composite RTM shell. Advantages include less weight (thinner-gauge steel required) and tighter fit (one-piece construction).

A second unique body feature is Viper's "world first" use of lightweight urethane foam for all structural interior trim panels. Another unique feature adds

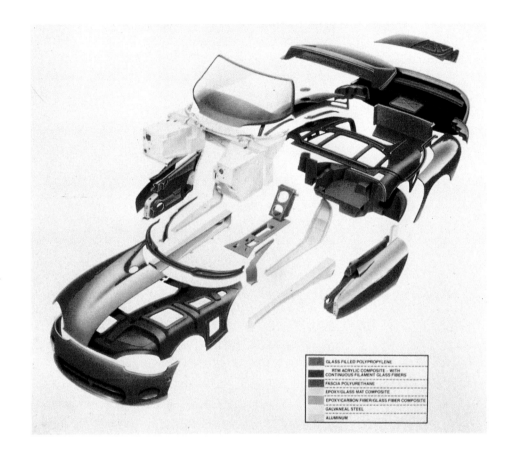

bumper beams that are constructed of foam-wrapped super-strength steel. Finally, Viper's "sportbar" houses a removable backlight for true flow-through ventilation. (However, the "sportbar" is not intended for roll-over support.)

Against such newfangled thinking, Viper manufacturing seems downright old-fashioned. You'll find no robots, no long conveyor lines, not even a paint

No car sold in the U.S. has more body panels formed by resin transfer molding (RTM), a time-saving method of creating high-quality composites. Also, the one-piece windshield frame combines steel and RTM surface material and extends into the passenger compartment to form the top of the instrument panel.

shop at the New Mack Avenue Viper Assembly plant: just a handful of "craftspersons," each trained to perform multiple, related tasks. All components arrive "just in time," Japanese-style. To ease production and to maintain consistent high quality, many major systems arrive fully assembled, including the entire No-nonsense cockpit's analog gauges turn from black-on-gray in daytime to yellow-on-orange at night. Air conditioning isn't offered by the factory.

underbody, engine, spring/shock units (from Koni/Rockwell), and the aforementioned wheel/brake systems. By design, body panels go on from the rear forward, and only after the chassis is completed, this to reduce the chance of in-plant body damage.

And that's the technical state of

"Bob Lutz's Cobra" as it enters the world in 1992. But what of tomorrow? Well, Team Viper is still together, working on what Lutz calls "possible enhancements" for the near term. Among these are roll-up windows, a driver's airbag, and a hard top (already designed, in fact) to supplement the fold-away top. Further down the road is the prospect of a fastback version like the sleek late-'60s Cobra

Daytona coupe. Intriguingly, a concept sketch for this very model adorns both Lutz's office and the Team Viper workroom.

At this point, Chrysler is definitely committed to "niche" vehicles like Viper—and perhaps more than one in any given year. Yet, the Viper we now know should

WARNING

Hot Exhaust Pipe Below Door Opening

AVOID CONTACTING
THIS AREA

CAUTION

Top Support Behind Seats is Not a Roll Bar
This is an Open Vehicle ‧‧ Drive Carefully

Read Owner's Manual for Additional
Important Safety Information

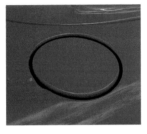

be around a good long while. Lutz explained: "This is a car that could easily live 10 years—if you don't overproduce. We'll continue to massage it, but I don't see it getting a 'mid-cycle restyle' any more than the Cobra ever did."

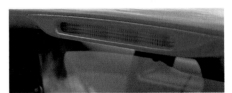

Still, it's certain there's more to come. "We want to get some experience with Viper in the marketplace," said design chief Tom Gale. "We've already learned from it regarding teamwork. But we've got the next [niche] project ready to go. As a matter of fact, we've got a couple to choose from. Whether it's Team Viper or some other team that will do it is something we're discussing. All I can say now is, 'Watch this space.'"

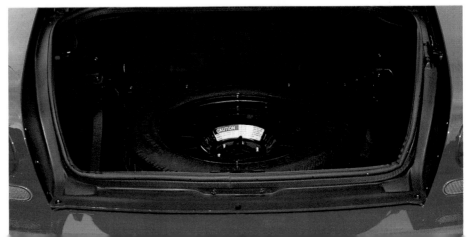

It was a poor time for a Japanese-made car to lead the most American of races. The Mitsubishi-built Dodge Stealth had been named to pace the 1991 Indianapolis 500, just as U.S. forces were going to war in the Persian Gulf. Chrysler had the perfect substitute. Viper.

Trouble was, Viper production was still months away and the only running examples were incomplete development cars. So Team Viper hand-built one. Begun in late February 1991, the car was at Indy for the May 4 opening ceremonies—with Carroll Shelby at the wheel.

This was great theater. Shelby, who had less than a year earlier undergone a heart transplant, rocketed giddy Chrysler insiders and adoring journalists around the Brickyard at 140 mph. Even in the rain. Even when the wipers weren't working. "Nobody could have enjoyed a car more than I did that month," Shelby said. The roadster gained exposure at the world's most-watched race, and Viper engineers gleaned reams of performance data.

Viper's next public appearance was on the streets of car-crazy Southern California, where Dodge put journalists into production numbers 5, 6, 11, and 14. The crimson caravan was a traffic-stopping, jaw-dropping sensation. Chrysler then loosed the quartet on Midtown Manhattan, where jaded New Yorkers swarmed like schoolkids.

Deliveries to dealers began during May of 1992, in unmarked trucks. To distribute the 196 1992 Vipers among its 2800 retailers, Chrysler identified the nation's top 40 markets for premium-priced sports cars (by checking the number of Corvette registrations), and pinpointed dealers based on sales and customer-satisfaction ratings.

The 1992 sticker showed a manufacturer's suggested retail price of $50,000, plus a $700 destination charge, a $2600 gas-guzzler tax, and a $2330 luxury tax, for a total of $55,630. Demand was so strong, however, that some dealers added $100,000 to the price, while buyers were bidding as high as $200,000. "If someone wants to pay a large amount of premium not to have to wait," Dodge Division General Manager Martin R. Levine said, "I don't have a problem with that." To ease the crunch, dealers were authorized to accept orders on the 3000 Vipers slated for production as 1993 models. By July 1992, some 70 percent were reportedly sold.

Viper's core buyers aren't the ultra-rich, but rather those of somewhat lesser means who tend to "spend a disproportionate amount of their income on automobiles," Levine said. Further, its lure isn't likely to be strongest among buyers of Ferraris or even Porsches, but among fans of classic American muscle. "If you realize what a big-block '67 Corvette goes for, you realize what a deal this car is," Levine explained. And while Chrysler's goal is to always build fewer Vipers than it can sell, speculators might be frustrated by the relatively open-ended production. "I think long-term, a Viper is going to be an amazing investment," Lutz explained. "But short-term, as production ramps up, I don't think the speculators are going to make money on it."

What is the nature of this machine they'll own?

It is a car best approached with caution. Cats-eye headlamps lead to libidinous haunches that burst with impossibly aggressive tires. The front fenders are cleaved open.

Side exhausts sneer at civility. The tail is fun-house-mirror wide. The Viper is where menace comes for lessons.

You unlatch the door by reaching inside for the plastic handle. Getting in isn't exceptionally difficult—as long as the top is off and you can simply drop into the buckets. To get out, you must hoist yourself over the wide door sill, which is likely to be quite hot from the exhaust pipe within. Dodge tried to keep the sill's surface temperature below 150 degrees; a sticker on the doorjamb warns you to avoid contact.

The driver's seat slides fore and aft, its backrest tilts, and a squeeze bulb pumps up the lumbar support. The seat is comfortable and properly bolstered for turns. The steering column adjusts vertically a few inches. Drilled to reduce weight, the pedals are offset to the left to clear the housing for the exhaust headers and transmission tunnel. There's no room for a deadpedal. Cockpit width is abundant and the footwells extend far forward, though the passenger's isn't wide enough to allow much variety in leg placement.

A speedometer and tachometer with black numerals on white faces straddle the steering wheel. A warning-light display is between them. Auxiliary gauges run across the upper center of the dashboard. A trio of simple knobs controls the heat/vent system. Just below is the Chrysler/Alpine stereo—two of its six speakers are in the vertical housing between the buckets. The stubby shifter is a handspan from the wheel rim. Only the parking brake lever, which sprouts from the wide center tunnel, is awkward to use.

Viper Versus Cobra

It is immediately apparent to those who have driven both the Viper and its inspiration, the AC Shelby Cobra 427, that they are indeed kindred spirits. Both are alive, intimidating—and have cockpits that get really hot.

But, as discovered by the editors of *Car and Driver*, the Cobra feels more feral than Viper. It has a wilder exhaust note, and is more of a challenge to rein in during aggressive driving.

Propelled by a 425-horsepower (gross) Ford V-8, the 2660-pound Cobra is marginally faster to 60 mph and in the quarter-mile than the 3400-pound, 400-horsepower (net) Viper. But the Dodge's superior aerodynamics and taller gearing allow it to storm ahead above 100 mph. Cobra's 4.11:1 axle ratio limited it to 134 mph at the 7000-rpm redline in the top of its four gears, while Viper's 3.07:1 helped it to 163 mph in fifth at 4900 rpm.

Skinnier tires, a narrower track, and slower steering combined to make the Cobra more of a challenge to drive all-out through turns. But Viper needed more shifting to stay quick around town.

The Cobra tested was an authentic 427SC newly produced by Carroll Shelby from original 1965-era chassis and parts. Its price is an estimated $500,000—and vintage Cobra 427s go for even more.

Unlike Cobra, which was built as a race car and sold as a road car merely to qualify for competition, Dodge has no plans to race the Viper (though unmodified examples would likely run in the Sports Car Club of America's top showroom-stock class against such cars as the LT-1 Corvette and Lotus Turbo Esprit).

Looking out over the hood and fender berms is quite reminiscent of the view from a Jaguar E-type. The low seating position itself doesn't hinder forward visibility, but there are no power mirrors, or even a convex right mirror, so you'll want to double check to make sure no traffic is obscured by the thick rear pillars. Unfortunately, a good portion of the dashtop is painted a highly reflective light-gray, which projects substantial glare onto the windshield when driving into the sun.

The 16-pound vinyl roof and side curtains stow atop the mini-spare

Snakes alive! Viper's first official public run was as pace car for the 1991 Indianapolis 500. Carroll Shelby drove.

tire in the small trunk, leaving little space for much more than a couple of bookbags. Interior storage is confined to the modestly sized glovebox and whatever one can squeeze in the narrow channel behind the seatbacks: There are no map pockets or storage bins.

Despite the heavily insulated floorboards, the footwells, particularly the driver's, grow oven-hot quickly and stay that way. Air

conditioning is a '93 dealer-installed option.

Viper's initial performance impression can be summed up in one word: T-O-R-Q-U-E. At just 1200 rpm, the big V-10 has 400 pounds/feet of it on tap. Nail it and the car catapults ahead from most any speed and in most any gear. There's uncanny flexibility here. Sixth gear at 55 mph shows just 1000 rpm, but you'll not notice any strain cruising at 65 in fifth. Shifting can become an afterthought. Anchor it in third to carve up mountain roads. Plant it in fourth to slice through freeway traffic.

There's no tangible gain from revving the V-10 within more than 1000 rpm of its 5600-rpm redline. Do so, however, and you unleash an alliance of exhaust moan and engine hiss almost frightening in tone and intensity. Troll in town, and Viper envelops you in a warm baritone burble. Accelerate at a

moderate cruising pace, however, and it bleats. If a Ferrari V-12's song is "ripping canvas," then a Viper at part-throttle is "ripping cardboard."

"That's one thing that I wish were different on the car," explained Chrysler President Bob Lutz, citing federal noise limits. "When you slide behind the wheel and twist the key, you're expecting race-car sounds. And when you stomp on it and take it up to the

redline, you wish for that full throaty cry of unbridled power. What you've got now is the unbridled power, but you really don't hear the exhaust; you just hear a rush of air. Having said that, you get used to it very quickly. Once you're accelerating in that thing, everything is forgotten."

Indeed, unleashing even a good portion of Viper's power when the front wheels aren't pointed straight will kick the tail out. And hard

acceleration on rutted or broken surfaces requires extra attention because the enormously wide front tires tend to seek out and follow pavement grooves or channels that otherwise go unnoticed.

Major controls—steering, clutch, brakes, shifter—demand firm, decisive inputs, but they're not tiring even in the constant use of city/suburban grinding. The clutch, in particular, proves surprisingly manageable, much more so than in the typical Corvette. And shift action is quick and direct. The second-gear lockout isn't so bothersome as the linkage's narrow gate, which requires extra concentration to slide the lever into the correct gear. Most troubling is that there is no reverse-gear lockout, so it is possible to inadvertently shift into reverse even while accelerating forward.

Steering is simply terrific: *very* responsive on initial tip-in, properly assisted for high-speed work, and always communicative. The brakes initially feel dead to the toes— heavy and with scant pedal travel—but they're discernibly powerful and fully up to the task of scrubbing off lots of speed quickly, consistently, and safely despite lacking ABS.

Viper's rapid, rain or shine. But erecting its foul-weather gear can be tedious. The side curtains attach separately and have zippered clear plastic flaps. You must "construct" the top before affixing it. The affair seals well, but traps engine heat for a sauna effect.

Dodge's newest supercar was an immediate hit in the scale-model world. Above: a 1/25-scale plastic promotional miniature by AMT Ertl. Below: Manufacturers of unassembled kits were quick to offer Vipers, as well.

Though grip is prodigious and body roll next to nil, the Viper demands a smooth touch. Abrupt throttle lift-off causes marked torque reaction or "rubber-banding" in the driveline that can combine with the stiff suspension to completely upset balance and send the car skittering into oversteer. Mid-corner rear-end

bump-steer is a problem too. No wonder the steering is so responsive; it has to be for recovery's sake, even with so much rubber on the road and near-perfect 50/50 weight distribution. Oversteer, of course, can be fun. But things can happen a lot faster in exotics than with everyday cars, so driving skill must be a match for the Viper's moves.

This racer-like demeanor doesn't translate into an overly harsh ride, though Viper is quite stiff through low-speed bumps. Its extremely rigid skeleton eliminates the structural flexing over pavement irregularities that afflicts so many convertibles. However, the huge

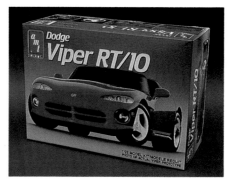

hood shudders over bumps, the plastic panels behind the cabin squeak, and at speeds over 50 mph, wind buffeting is intense.

Rain causes its own comfort problems. Slotting in each side curtain is a snap, but the toupee-like top? First, spread the longitudinal outriggers to form a basic frame, then connect them with three cross-braces. Next, plug the prongs at the rear of that assembly into receptacles atop the "sportbar," and finally cinch down the front with two latches at the windshield header. The top seals well and doesn't restrict headroom, but it also traps all that engine heat. The cabin rapidly turns into a sauna. High humidity mists the inside of the windshield. The curtains, which can't be removed on the go, have zippered flaps for convenience, but they won't stay open for ventilation at anything above a crawl. Even then, they open only about halfway.

Still, it's all part of the back-to-basics Viper experience. "As soon as somebody says, 'Why not roll-up windows?' you know immediately this car is not for them," remarked Chrysler spokesman Thomas J. Kowaleski. "When we launched it in California, one of the people at

Viper wares such as this lavish color dealer brochure (*left*), the Indy media kit (*below*), and a folder distributed to the press (*bottom*) are already of interest to collectors.

the hotel was Regis Philbin—you know, Regis and Kathy Lee? I introduced myself and said, 'We're out here launching this car, you ought to come down and see it.' So that night he comes down, and he takes one look at it and says 'Where's the door handles? You think anybody's gonna buy a car without door handles?' And I say, 'Regis, this is not for you.' And his car comes out of the valet, and it was an old Cadillac Seville. Two days later, Nicolas Cage, the actor, drives into the hotel in a Corvette, and just literally on a dead run comes over to the Viper. He understood immediately."

"This," explained Dodge chief Levine, "is a no-excuses car for no-excuses people."